RELIGIONS OF HUMANITY

Above: The Temple Mount in Jerusalem.

Left: Faithful praying at the Wailing Wall, the remains of the Temple that was rebuilt in the first century B.C.E. on the original ancient site. It is a place venerated by the Jews. It evokes the roots of their religious history.

Facing page: A Torah scroll (from the Synagogue in Madrid, Spain).

Chelsea House Publishers
1974 Sproul Road, Suite 400, Broomall, PA 19008
The Chelsea House world wide web address is www.chelseahouse.com

English-language edition
© 2002 by Chelsea House Publishers, a subsidiary of Haights Cross Communications
All rights reserved.

First Printing

1 3 5 7 9 6 4 2

Library of Congress Cataloging-in-Publication Data Applied For:
ISBN: 0-7910-6630-4

© 2000 by Editoriale
Jaca Book spa, Milan
All rights reserved.
Originally published by
Editoriale Jaca Book, Milan, Italy
Design by Jaca Book
Original English text by
Lawrence E. Sullivan

LAWRENCE E. SULLIVAN

THE RELIGIOUS TRADITION OF
JUDAISM

CHELSEA HOUSE PUBLISHERS
PHILADELPHIA

CONTENTS

INTRODUCTION

"YOU WILL BE MY PEOPLE, AND I WILL BE YOUR GOD"

Judaism is the way Jews of the Hellenistic world described their manner of serving God. Other Jews at other times and places have used different terms, which some prefer today. Still, Judaism is the term used widely and respectfully by most Jews and non-Jews alike to designate the religious life of Israel, God's holy people. Judaism, in all its varieties, is a way of life observed by Jewish people for nearly 3,300 years, beginning when God chose Abraham, the ancestral Father of Israel, from among all the nations. The Jewish people consider themselves descendants of Abraham and Sarah, Isaac and Rebekah, and Jacob and Leah and Rachel, Bilhah and Zilpah.

Judaism is dedicated to observance of the Torah, a word that means "teaching." Torah refers to all of the Hebrew Bible, especially the Pentateuch (the first five books), as well as to the oral teachings and lore that comprise Jewish tradition. Two forms of Torah, one written and the other oral, emerge from the Covenant relationship God established with the people of Israel through Moses around 1200 B.C.E.

Today the culture of Judaism flowers in the realm of ideas, sciences, professions, and the arts, leaving an impressive mark on human history today, as it has for millennia. Throughout the world there are about 17 million Jews, of whom more than 7 million live in North America, over 3.7 million in Israel, and some 3.5 million in Europe and states of the former Soviet Union.

Outside of the Jewish community few are familiar with its rich and varied religious traditions. Relations between Jews and non-Jews have suffered because of this ignorance. Throughout their history Jews have born the brunt of misunderstanding and persecution precisely for being who they are: their defining adherence to their religious lifeways and their faithfulness to their distinctive covenant with God. In opening a book on Judaism, readers do well to recall that little more than fifty years ago, from 1937 until 1945, there was a systematic attempt in Europe to completely exterminate the Jewish people using the full force and fury of the modern nation-state. There is a pressing need to know Judaism better.

Jewish religious life is an extraordinary one; it stands out in human history. To understand how Jews have constantly reshaped their way of life around faithfulness to the God who has chosen them turns one away from blind prejudice toward an enriching appreciation. Given the historical depth and social complexity of Judaism, and given the many different ways that Jews themselves describe their core beliefs and practices, this short book aims only to sketch a brief outline of a few important events and ideas.

Facing page: The remains of the Synagogue of Gamla, known for its valiant resistance against Rome in 68 C.E. It is located a few miles east of the Sea of Galilee, which lies at the conjunction of the Golan Heights, the Galilee, and the Jordan Valley. Right: A Jewish family out for a walk in Brooklyn, New York.

1
"BAR MITZVAH": BECOMING SUBJECT TO THE COMMANDMENTS

This boy is undergoing his *bar mitzvah*, an important ceremony in his life and in the life of his community. *Bar mitzvah,* meaning "son of the commandment," is the name of a ritual observed when a Jewish boy reaches the age of thirteen years plus one day. (A similar celebration, called the *bat mitzvah*, is celebrated among some Jews for the girls who have reached twelve years plus one day in age). The boy's family and friends celebrate his passage into responsibility for study, prayer, and observance of the law. They also celebrate the renewal of the community and the transmission of the Torah to a new generation. For the first time, the boy rises to recite the words of Torah before the congregation in worship. The scroll is taken out of the ark and opened to the proper section for the day. The boy intones the ancient Hebrew Scripture in the traditional manner and addresses an interpretation to the congregation. As signs and reminders of his resposibilities, he receives the *tallit*, or prayer shawl, and *tefillin*, two small leather containers holding passages from Exodus (13:1-10 and 13:11-16) and words from the *Shema* (Deuteronomy 6:4-9; and 11:13-21). One of the *tefillin* (meaning "prayers") is fixed on his head with a leather strap; the other is bound to the upper part of his left arm (if he is right-handed), opposite the heart. From now on, dressed and equipped as an attendant of the Divine King in his court, the young man counts as one who can form a *minyan*, the group of at least ten men required to form a synagogue community for worship.

Mitzvot (plural, "commandments") play a major role in the life and identity of Jews as individuals and as community members. Even *mitzvot* developed in rabbinical teaching derive their authority and creative power from God (Deuteronomy 17: 9-11). All commandments stem from the Torah God has revealed. The rabbis remarked on some 613 commandments given to the chosen people in the Torah, including the Decalogue given to Moses on Mount Sinai. They took note as well of seven universal *mitzvot* given to all humankind in the days of Noah. Given that all of life is to be lived under God's command many halakhic norms are considered *mitzvot*. Certain areas of life stand out as especially marked by *mitzvot* that characterize Jewish life: circumcision of males; prayer; keeping Sabbath as a holy day; sexual relations and marriage; study of Torah; food and diet; the *mezuzah* (small receptacle that contains hand-written biblical passages on parchment) that marks the doorway to a Jewish home and other doorways within; festivals (*chagim*); and *tzedakah*, a word that literally means "uprightness" or "righteousness" and refers especially to generous contributions to charity, avoidance of gossip, and comforting of mourners.

Scenes from an open-air bar mitzvah in Jerusalem. In the large photograph, the young man is wearing tefillin (small leather boxes containing Shema' Israel, the consummate Jewish prayer). Placed on the forehead and left arm during prayers, they indicate that the mind and the heart are with God. Having been taught by the rabbi, the young man will be able to publicly read the Scriptures.

2
ISRAEL, THE HOLY PEOPLE OF GOD: BIBLICAL FOUNDATIONS

The religious life of Judaism is rooted in the life and history of the Hebrew people, who first appear in history as nomadic tribes moving through the upper regions of the Arabian desert, in the shadows and margins of the great empires of Egypt, Sumer, Akkad, and Phoenicia.

The life of the Hebrew people, beginning with the call of Abraham after 2000 B.C.E., is recorded in the Hebrew Bible, whose Pentateuch (first five books) was compiled after the destruction of the Temple in 586 B.C.E. and in response to captivity in Babylon (586–538 B.C.E.). The people of Israel returned from exile in the years 538 to 515 B.C.E. and, drawing on a variety of sources, composed most of the Hebrew Bible as we know it during that and the following period (538–333 B.C.E.). The Pentateuch, known also as the Torah of Moses, therefore reflects the pattern of Israel's experience of exile from and return to Israel (seen also as the suffering caused by alienation from God and the reconciliation marked by renewal of right relationship with God). In this light the Hebrew Bible tells the story of the Exodus of the Israelites from Egypt, led by Moses, around 1260 B.C.E., the settlement of twelve tribes in Canaan, and the establishment of a kingship, led first by Saul and then by David, from the southern tribe of Judah, who established Jerusalem as a religious center. There David installed the Ark of the Covenant and his son Solomon (961–922 B.C.E.) built the fabulous Temple. Later the nation split into two kingdoms, Israel in the North and Judah in the south. These were conquered by Assyria (in 722 B.C.E.) and Babylon (in 587 B.C.E.) and the temple of Solomon was destroyed. The pattern of exile and return, well established in the time of Ezra (450 B.C.E.), framed an abiding inquiry about how best to observe the covenantal conditions that God set forth in giving the land to the chosen people. One outcome of the constant inquiry was an abundant and varied Jewish religious literature, including a translation of the Torah into Greek (250–200 B.C.E.).

The fact that Torah includes methods for inquiry and ongoing development is essential, for it means that the traditions of Torah are open-ended and remain the responsibility of each successive new generation in history. Defining Torah as ongoing inquiry changes the nature of reading the Bible: not only is the Bible the story of the Hebrew people and their relationship with God, but it is also a story about the revelatory nature of existence in time. The eternal being of God enters a vital relationship with his finite creatures of temporal existence. God reveals his purposes in the world of time, through the changes and struggles of his chosen people in history, especially in the unique and unrepeatable events of salvation that disclose his law and teaching. Key figures of the Hebrew

2

1. The background of this page is the desert, the dramatic symbol of where humans encounter both God and temptations; it witnessed the exodus of the Israelites from Egypt.
2. In the circle, several great Jewish symbols can be found: the Ark of the Covenant; the seven-branched candelabrum (menorah)—its central branch represents the Sabbath, God's day, the other branches represent the other six days of the creation—; the rams horn, which begins celebrations; and stylized trees, symbols of fertility (from a glass pan at the Israel Museum, Jerusalem).

Bible—Adam, Noah, Abraham, Moses, Nehemiah—appear in distinct circumstances of major significance: the Garden of Eden, the Universal Flood, the Exodus from Egypt, the Captivity in Babylon, the restoration of the Temple. God reveals Himself in His extraordinary deeds, exemplified by the way He raised His mighty hand to lead the people out of Egypt (Deuteronomy 6:22). History was reviewed and recorded in the Bible in light of God's extraordinary actions in history. In promising to be faithful to His people and in insisting that they review the meaning of His will in all circumstances, God thus transforms the life of the observant inquirer in each generation into a manifestation of His will and an event of salvation history.

3. The drawing, based on the description found in the Book of Kings, depicts the great Temple built by King Solomon, whose reign marks the period of maximum splendor in the history of Israel. With this memorable work, Solomon brings to completion the plans of his father King David.

4. At the time of David and Salomon, two sages of Israel discuss putting into written form the events that led to the establishment of the Jewish people and monarchy. Such events had been transmitted orally to them by their ancestors through many generations. These sages also recall the history of humanity since the oldest times: they gather ancient traditions from other peoples they had come in contact with, yet reworking their contents in the light of their own specific religious experience. Since the tenth century until the sixth-fifth century B.C.E., while the Jews were in exile, several narrations were assembled which later became the Jewish Bible.

3
DIASPORA

Diaspora means "dispersion," referring to the way in which Jewish people became scattered like seeds, far from the land of Israel. Early Jewish records take note of those who serve God while living outside the Land of Israel in the midst of peoples who worship other deities. Such was the experience of Abraham in the last days of the Sumerian kingdom and that of Moses in Egypt, called to lead the chosen people toward the Promised Land, which he never entered.

In 587 B.C.E. Jerusalem fell and Jews entered captivity in Babylon. Some returned 50 years later, but others stayed to form a Jewish community within Babylonian society. When Alexander the Great "conquered the world" two centuries later, Jews further dispersed throughout his empire, taking residence, for example, in Alexandria. Jewish scholars there translated the Bible into Greek. Other emigrants settled in Antioch, Rome, and the cities of the Greco-Roman world. Throughout the Hellenistic world, Jews preserved their faith by forming synagogue congregations that studied and obeyed the Torah, supported the Temple in Jerusalem, abided by decisions of the *Sanhedrin* there, and made pilgrimages to Jerusalem if possible. Jewish intellectuals, like Philo Judaeus (20 B.C.E. - 50 C.E.) read Greek and Roman philosophy in the light of faith and vice versa. After the fall of Jerusalem in 70 C.E. and its destruction in 135 C.E. Jews entered a period of great dispersion throughout the wider world.

Jewish life reflects the experience of Diaspora. In addition to use of the major literary languages of Hebrew, Greek and Latin, and the many languages of the lands inhabited by Jewish minorities, for instance, there evolved specifically Jewish languages whose sounds were written down using letters from the Hebrew alphabet but whose languages arose from unrelated vernaculars such as Judeo-Arabic, Judeo-Persian, Ladino, and Yiddish, in lands where Jews lived. Diverse influences are reflected in Jewish practice. For example, in traditional prayer life (as after a lesson of Talmudic study), the *Kaddish* ("sanctification" prayer for the Lord's return to His people and His temple) is recited not in Hebrew but in Aramaic, reflecting the days of the Second Commonwealth and rabbinic period.

Although Jews often made prominent contributions to the societies in which they lived, they remained minorities. Their treatment at the hands of rulers and populace alike was often based on misunderstanding and open hatred. They were repressed by law and on many occasions massacred in large numbers, as occurred in York in 1190 and in association with the outbreaks of plague in 1348. Notwithstanding moments of fruitful interaction with non-Jews, Jews frequently became targets of injustice, expulsion, and persecution. They were formally expelled from Spain in 1492 and from Portugal in 1497, causing these Jews, called Sefardim, to scatter to the Middle East, North Africa, Holland, Northern Europe, and South America. These expulsions echoed earlier ones of Ashkenazi Jews from Lithuania (1495) and Germany (1348-1350) into Poland.

In the span of seven years, from 1938 to 1945, six million

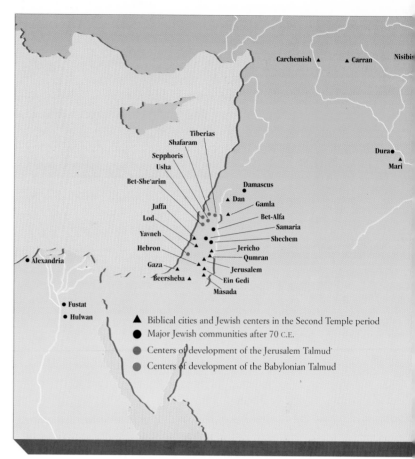

1. The centers of ancient Judaism.
2. Judaism in southern Europe and North Africa.
3. Judaism in Asia.
4. The Jewish Diaspora, estimates for 1984. Thin line: less than 250,000; thick line: 250,000 or more. 1) USA 5.72 million; 2) Canada 330,000; 3) France 670,000; 4) United Kingdom 360,000; 5) Argentina 250,000; 6) Brazil 130,000; 7) Hungary 75,000; 8) Mexico 40,000; 9) Uruguay 44,000; 10) Venezuela 17,000; 11) Australia 70,000; 12) Republic of South Africa 105,000; 13) India 7,000; 14) Ethiopia 18,000; 15) Iran 35,000; 16) Italy 35,000; 17) Turkey 21,000; 18) Syria 4,000; 19) Morocco 17,000; 20) The Former Soviet Union 1.76 million; 21) Romania 30,000; 22) Switzerland 21,000; 23) The Netherlands 28,000; 24) Belgium 41,000; 25) Germany 42,000; 26) Spain 13,000.
5. The Ark of the Covenant and other Jewish symbols. The drawing is from a window decorated in gold in the Israel Museum, Jerusalem.

Jews were deliberately killed for being Jews; one third of the world's Jewish population was exterminated. Whether and how the meaning of such an event can be attained in the light of election by God are matters of grave concern and debate in Judaism today.

Messianic themes of various sorts—from political redemption to spiritual renewal—are reflected in Zionism, the movement that facilitated the return of Jews to Palestine in the modern period. Throughout the centuries of Diaspora, Jews nourished the hope of return to Israel. When that hope based in scripture merged with the rise of 19th century nationalism, it found expression in the writings of Moses Hess and Theodor Herzl. In 1896, in response to growing anti-Semitism, Herzl published *The Jewish State* and organized a Zionist Congress in 1897. The nation state of Israel was established in 1948.

▲ Nineveh

▲ Asshur

Hamadan •

Pumbeditha
Baghdad •
Mahoza
Nehardea • Mata Mehasya
Sura
Babylon

Susa ▲

Ur ▲

Basra •

• Tbilisi
Cairo • Damascus • • Ukbarah • Khiva
Baghdad • • Nihavand • Moshhad
Jerusalem • Basra • • Qumisi
Khotan • Kaifeng •
Gonder • • Sa'na
• Aden
Canton •
• Bombay
Cranganore • • Madras
Cochin

● Major Jewish communities
— The Silk Route

Orange
Posquières • Turin
Biarritz • Lunel • Avignon Mantua Padua • • Venice
Bayonne • Montpellier • Aix
Narbonne • Genoa • Ferrara
Tudela • Perpignan • Lucca • • Split
Marseilles • Florence
Lisbon • Tortosa • Livorno • Pisa • Cattaro
Toledo • Gerona • Rome • Nicopolis
Barcelona • Naples Durazzo • Adrianople • Constantinople
Cordoba • Capua Salonika • • Gallipoli
Granada • Otranto • Kastoria • Abydos
Arzila • Palermo Smyrna •
Oran • Algiers • Bizerta Catania • Messina Patras • Mastaura
Fez • Syracuse Modon • Ephesus
Debdou • Tlemcen Tunis • Athens
Kairouan • Coron •
Rissani • Nefta • Gabès
Tripoli •
Misurata • Ptolemais
Sirte • Alexandria •
Cairo •

● Major Jewish communities
● Major centers of resettlement after the
  expulsion from Spain and Portugal

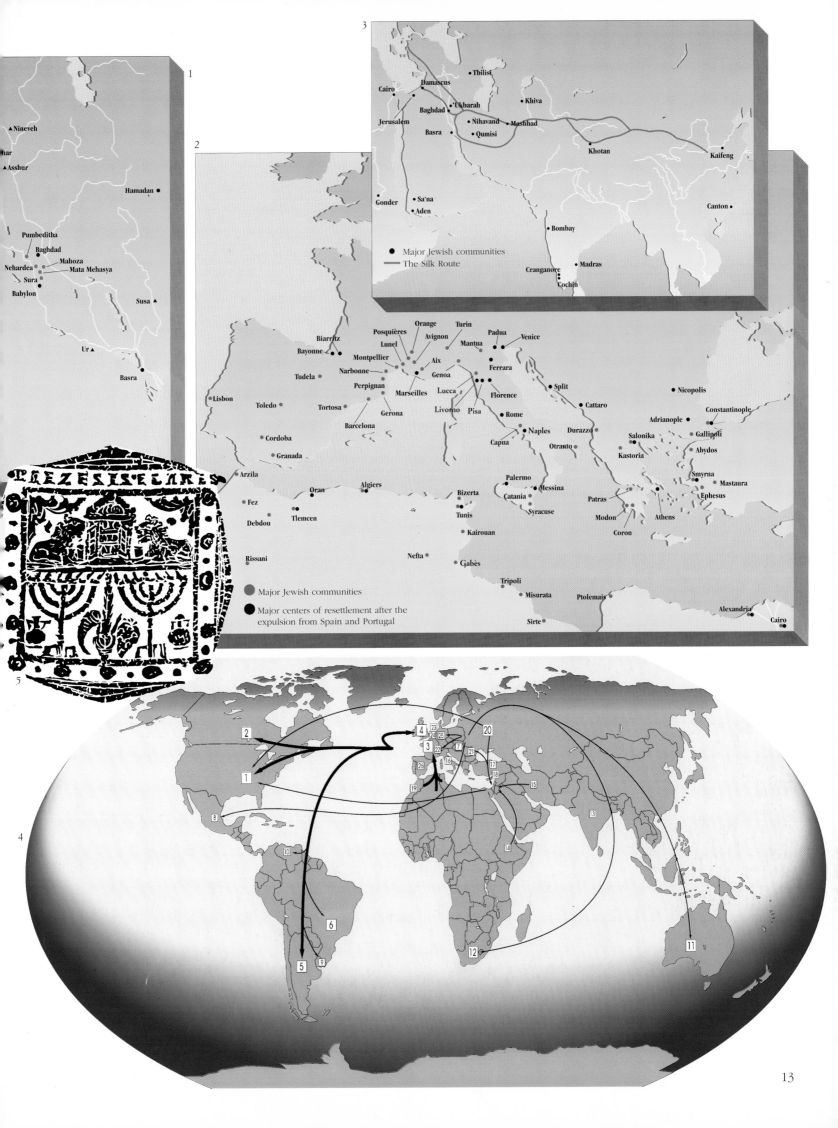

ELECTION: GOD'S CHOSEN PEOPLE

"The Lord God has chosen you to be a people for his own possession" (Deuteronomy 7:6). God's selection of Abraham was renewed with his descendants, the people of Israel, throughout history. Faithful to His promises, the signs of election appear throughout Israel's history. The Lord spared the lives of Israel's first-born when the heads of all other lineages in Egypt were visited by death and plagued by destruction. The Lord chose to set them free from bondage in Egypt; elected to reveal to them his own nature, name, and will at Sinai; agreed to establish a kingship in Jerusalem and set that city as a light to the nations, beaming like a sanctuary lamp in the world-temple He had created. It was the Lord who renewed His election of Israel after exile, signified by the reconstruction of the Temple and the renewal of His Covenant.

Religious Jews know themselves to be a people set apart by election and Torah, the will of the God they serve: not an impersonal force of nature nor a first principle of philosophy, but a divine personality with a revealed name, the source of all holiness and uprightness, who created in the beginning an orderly and good universe and revealed in time His commands about action within it. Above all, Jews are a people set apart by the one and only God who chose them by name in a singular way. God entered a special relationship with them, a covenant agreement binding on both parties. Out of reverence, ancient Jewish custom avoids pronouncing directly the name of God revealed to Moses: YHWH or the double *yud* in Hebrew, which comes to be pronounced not as written but as *Adonai* meaning "My Lord."

The meaning of chosenness has been a constant question in Judaism. During certain periods, Jews remained faithful to their election by separating the community from the corruption of neighboring religions. At other times, as in Europe from the 12th to the 18th centuries, gentiles in the majority forced Jews to live in walled ghettos with gates locked at night. How Jews should maintain the distinctiveness that signals their election today is a question among Jews, religious or secular. The varying answers to that question have, in part, given rise to several branches of practice discussed in Chapter Nine. Judaism is not primarily a set of beliefs. Jews do not say a common creed, for instance. There exists a general mandate to think broadly and debate interpretations. Rather, Judaism emphasizes concrete practice to observe God's will: rite, custom (*minhag*), and a life ordered by the Torah. An observant Jew unites a life of necessary actions with a life of religious practice in line with God's intention in electing Israel: to elevate all of the benefits of life to the level of holiness, to sanctify them by uniting them with God's will.

A major instrument for hallowing the world is the religious calendar that begins with *R'osh ha-Shanah*, New Year, in late September. The first ten days of the year are for penance and reflection and the tenth day is known as *Yom Kippur*, the Day of Atonement, emphasizing repentance and forgiveness. In autumn *Succoth*, the festival of booths, recalls Israel's time of wandering in the wilderness and, at the same time, celebrates with thanksgiving the fruitfulness of the earth. In mid-winter, at the eight-day festival of *Hanukkah* (Dedication) also known as the Feast of Lights, Jews celebrate the ritual cleansing of the temple at Jerusalem in 165 B.C.E. after a revolt by the Maccabee brothers obtained religious freedom. Each night they light an additional candle on the *hanukkiyya* to commemorate the miracle when a small cruet of oil burned for eight nights. In late winter or early spring, the carnival-like feast of *Purim* (lots) celebrates the victory of the Jews of Persia over Haman, who advised the enemy king. The *megilla* (scroll of Esther) is chanted in the synagogue, to the accompaniment of much deliberate noise and merrymaking, especially whenever Haman's name is mentioned. The religious year is renewed in *Pesach*, Passover, in the spring, commemorating the liberation of the people of Israel from captivity in Egypt. The principal celebration takes the form of a ritualized meal where family and friends read and talk about the story of Israel's deliverance. The gathering of Passover resembles also the symposium held in the ancient Greek world, where philosophers (literally, "lovers of wisdom") assembled at a meal to probe and experience issues of deepest concern. *Shavuot* ("weeks") occurs fifty days after *Pesach* to commemorate the Giving of the Torah on Mount Sinai. In addition to these feasts, many Jews observe at least five day-long fasts throughout the year, especially on *Tish b'Ab* (the ninth day of the month of Ab), which commemorates the day Babylonians destroyed the first Temple and Romans destroyed the second. The primary emphasis in ceremonial life is to observe the command "to remember and not to forget" God's saving interactions with Israel.

Current debate about election and observance is animated by increasing rates of intermarriage between Jews and gentiles and by trends toward secularization in modern society. Talk of election and its meaning is shadowed by the unspeakable event of the Holocaust.

1. In the background: tradition dating back to Helen, the mother of Emperor Constantine, identifies this as Mount Sinai. From a 19th century lithograph by David Roberts.
4. Today, Sinai, the sacred mountain, symbol of the pact between God and the people of Israel, is the subject of archeological research. Having led numerous excavations into this area, the prehistorical scholar Emmanuel Anati hypothesized that the holiness of the mountain dates back to the Paleolithic Era, placing Mount Sinai in the Negev Desert and identifying it as the mountain Har Karkom.

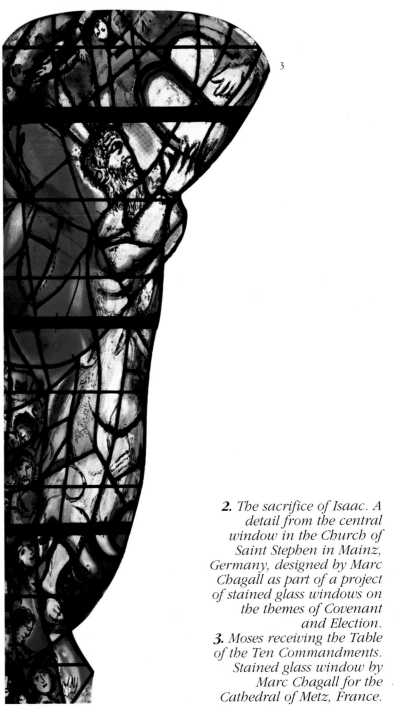

2. *The sacrifice of Isaac. A detail from the central window in the Church of Saint Stephen in Mainz, Germany, designed by Marc Chagall as part of a project of stained glass windows on the themes of Covenant and Election.*
3. *Moses receiving the Table of the Ten Commandments. Stained glass window by Marc Chagall for the Cathedral of Metz, France.*

SOURCES OF THE TORAH: LAW, TEACHING, AND OBSERVANCE

One view of the TORAH, meaning God's will for the Jewish people, refers to tradition transmitted in an unbroken chain from Moses to Joshua, to the Hebrew elders and prophets, to leaders like Ezra and Nehemiah of the mid-fifth century B.C.E., to the earliest rabbis mentioned in the Talmud. A different view of Torah, sometimes called a liberal one, sees the tradition develop over time, blending faithfulness to what was received from the past with creativity to the changing circumstances of present and future. Either view of Torah's revelation and transmission recognizes certain authoritative expressions of Torah that stand out above others. The twenty-four books of the Hebrew Bible form three sections: the Torah (the *Pentateuch* or first five books); *Neviim* (the Prophets) and *Ketuvim* (Writings or Hagiography). The written Torah refers especially to the first five books of the Bible, which are also simply called the Law of Moses. By the mid-fifth century B.C.E., the reading of written Torah was a central feature of public worship (Nehemiah 9:3). Torah also includes oral teachings that are both legal and nonlegal in character as well as methods for ongoing development of the Torah tradition.

Next to the Bible, the TALMUD is the classic text of Judaism, an authoritative source of tradition and the principle text of rabbinic Judaism. There exist two Talmuds, both written in the Aramaic language. The Talmud is rabbinical commentary on the Mishnah (dealing with less than 40 of the 63 treatises in the Mishnah, however, it does not comment on all six orders of the Mishnah). The Talmud Yerushalmi (called the Jerusalem or Palestinian Talmud) was composed at the end of the fourth century C.E. The Babylonian Talmud, longer and more ambitious in scope, was edited at the end of the fifth century C.E. and is more authoritative. The two broad headings of most Talmudic concerns are: *Halakhah* (dealing with law, rite, and customary practice); and *Aggadah* (dealing with theological and ethical argument as well as narrative and folklore).

The MISHNAH is a topic law code in six parts with 63 subdivisions and formed over a long time, which, some believe, extends back in the Near East to the time before the formation of the Bible and reaching forward to the second century C.E. Tradition attributes compilation to Rabbi Judah the Prince, the patriarch of the Jewish community of Palestine. The Mishnah authority lies in revelation alongside the Pentateuch: it describes itself (in the tractate *Abot* regarding founders and their sayings) as an expression of Torah revealed on Sinai and transmitted *in oral form* from the time of Moses until its inscription in the Mishnah. Its message: behind all the hierarchical manifestations, seen in the great chain of being in the world, lies the one, true, and holy God. In practice, the Mishnah is an authoritative source for rabbinic teaching and inquiry in Tannaitic, or early rabbinic, Judaism. The Mishnah's view of holiness and sanctification reflects priestly and

1. In this stained glass window from the Cathedral in Metz, Marc Chagall depicts Moses in front of the burning bush and expresses the power of the Divine Calling.
2. From a Jewish manuscript of the 12th century, we see the signature of Moses ben Maimon, known as Maimonides.
3. 4. The bronze bust of Maimonides. The statue, a work by A. Ostrzega, can be found at Hebrew University on Mount Scopus, Jerusalem. Here the figure of the philosopher is placed along the Nile to indicate that when he lived in the great Egyptian city of Cairo at the end of the 12th century, all the Jews of the predominantly Islamic countries along the Mediterranean and the Middle East turned to him as their sage.

הונה מספרי אתי מ?מא כרבי מימון

Levitical concepts rooted in Temple rite and calendar, as reflected upon by philosophical sages after the Roman destruction of the Temple.

Many other written works, too numerous to mention, influence tradition. They include: the commentary on the Bible and Talmud by Solomon ben Isaac, known as Rashi (1040-1105), and two works by the philosopher Moses Maimonides (1135–1204), known as Rambam. His *Mishneh Torah* ("review of the Torah") organized Jewish law and included issues basic to faith, such as conditions for the messianic age. And

5. *"Sefer" Torah, the scroll on which the Pentateuch is transcribed. The Synagogue Or Hachaim in Jerusalem, where this scroll is housed, has kindly allowed us to photograph it.*
6. *A page from a Russian Talmud from the last century.*

Maimonides' *The Guide for the Perplexed* reworked Jewish theology in the light of Aristotle. Later Rabbi Joseph Caro (1488-1575) prepared *Shulchan Arukh* (The "Prepared Table") the most influential code of law and ritual, which includes customs from Spanish and Middle Eastern life. Rabbi Moses Isserles (1525-1572) added customs of central and eastern Europe.

AUTHORITY: PROPHET, PRIEST, TEACHER

The authority that guides and governs the religious life of the Jewish community has changed over time, in regard to form, function, and spiritual emphasis. The prophet, the priest, and the rabbi ("teacher") exemplify shifts in authority that mark various epochs of Judaism.

PROPHET. The Biblical prophets spoke for God in order to challenge the state of affairs on earth. Several kinds of prophets appeared, especially from the eighth to the sixth centuries B.C.E. when they played a central role in Israel. Bands of unnamed wandering prophets, associated with King Saul and his madness, deliberately induced ecstasy through dance and music. Other kinds of prophets like Elijah or Nathan confronted Kings with dramatic oral statements that questioned the moral caliber of the King's own actions. Still other prophets like Amos, Jeremiah, and Isaiah composed written analyses of injustice, inequity, abuse of power, decadence, and religious hypocrisy. The prophets insisted on a life of genuine observance of God's commands, especially the command that humans establish justice, mercy, and holiness throughout the land and that kings foster the wellbeing even of their lowliest subjects. At times courageous prophets announced God's decision to rebuke His wayward people in order to instruct them by means of calamity and defeat at the hands of enemy nations (Amos 3:2). Assyria sacked the Northern Kingdom in 722 B.C.E. and Nebuchadnezzar of Babylonia carried the leaders of the Southern Kingdom into exile in 587. During such destructions, captivities, and exiles, the prophets steadfastly announced that the faithful remnant of Israel would be set free and vindicated.

PRIEST. When Ezra the scribe, leading some 1,700 Babylonian Jews back to Jerusalem after captivity, assembled the people to renew the spiritual life of the community, he read them a book of the law. They bound themselves to observe its codes of holiness and place the priests of the temple at the center of their renewed religious life. A new state was begun with power vested in the priests, an office with roots in ancient Israel. To this day, lineages of priests (*kohen*, pl. *kohanim*) can be traced. The high priest was descended from Zadok, the priest appointed in King David's time. Living in the Temple at Jerusalem, the high priest ruled both the state and the religious life of the nation. Religious life became highly centralized around the temple and also around the calendar of festivals and fasts. Above all, religious life revolved around the priests, Levites, and scribes who functioned there. The priests and scribes centered on the temple undertook a massive literary effort, particularly in the fifth century B.C.E., copying and compiling writings of prophets, old and new, and composing complete Biblical works that expanded, revised, and added materials drawn from a variety of sources and genres. Eventually the schools of scribes would give rise to the learned Pharisaic schools and their rabbis of the first century B.C.E. The Pharisees, in turn, produced the works of

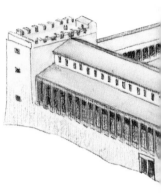

Two great prophets in Jewish religious history are represented by Marc Chagall in the stained glass windows of the Union Church in Pocantico Hills (Tarrytown, New York).
1. Isaiah depicted while an angel purifies his lips in order to announce the word of God.
2. Jeremiah, having warned the people of the Babylonian conquest and denounced their arid religiosity, is incarcerated as a defeatist.

teaching, writing, and legal inquiry that would guide Jewish life for the millennia after the destruction of the Temple.

RABBI. After the destruction of the Second Temple of Jerusalem in 70 C.E., authority shifted away from the Temple-based priests who presided over rites of sacrifice to the teachers (rabbis) directing study of Torah. In turn, the synagogues where Jews assembled to study under a rabbi became central to worship. Indeed, the Talmudic texts edited in the fourth and fifth centuries organize and elevate study in such a way as to transform the process of human inquiry into a form of worship and interpretation into an extension of God's revelation. Under rabbinic authority Jews fused rigorous questioning with pious devotion to constitute a single process of religious life, one that maintains its vitality and focus after two thousand years.

א טוב

3. 4. In the background, a drawing of the reconstructed Temple in Jerusalem, as was Herod the Great's desire. He is the one who began the imposing work around 20 B.C.E., and ten years later solemnly inaugurated the completion of the work. In the foreground, various individuals whose functions are tied to the Temple. In addition to the prophets, the other prominent religious figures for the people of Israel were the priests, who always had played an important role because they presided at Temple functions and, according to Jewish norms, were required to explain the Holy Scriptures to the people. But the sages and the scribes, students of the Law, over time had taken these teaching duties away from the priests.

5. A miniature representing a marriage, taken from one of the most important Jewish books on laws and customs written in Toledo, Spain, at the beginning of the 14th century. This book was often copied and, at times, illustrated. This scene is from a manuscript from Mantova, Italy, first half of the 15th century, which was meant for a rabbi. The rabbi was assuming, within Jewish religious life, an ever-increasing authority, based on his devotion and erudition.

7
MESSIANISM

Prophetic sayings that originally referred to the kings of the ancient Kingdom of Judah gave rise to speculation concerning a Messiah, the righteous king whom God would choose to overthrow wicked oppressors and rule Jews and the wider world with justice and mercy. The Hebrew word *mashiach*, means "the anointed one." In the Bible the title indicated kings, high priests, or those elevated to places of honor. From the time of the Babylonian Captivity, "messiah" designated especially the one who will redeem God's chosen people from oppression, exile, suffering, and degradation. Acting as a mighty warrior, the Messianic King would lead his chosen people in battle and fulfil the other authoritative roles of prophet, priest, and teacher described in chapter six. At the same time, the value of suffering became increasingly clear over the course of Biblical history, especially through the preaching of the prophets.

After the Second Temple of Jerusalem was destroyed in 70 C.E., the title "Messiah" denoted the one who will gather up Jews from their dispersion in the Diaspora. Exactly how such salvation would be achieved has been a matter of great excitement and discussion. Was the Messiah to be a political figure elevating the nation of chosen people over their enemies on the world stage? Was he to be a spiritual leader renewing the moral purity and force of the chosen people? Was the scale of the Messiah's accomplishment to be national, worldwide, or even cosmic? Would God Himself intervene directly as the messianic agent in human history to create conditions of freedom, moral order, and happiness, or would the messiah be a human leader? Would the transformations brought by the Messiah create a world never seen before or restore a condition that already existed, for example, in the time of King David? In fact, would the Messianic Age dawn in this world or only after this world is brought to an end?

Since the dawn of the Messianic age is signaled by trial, persecution, and suffering, and since Jews have often suffered such circumstances in history, no age has had its shortage of self-proclaimed messiahs. Christianity began as a Jewish movement declaring Jesus the messiah. Soon afterward, in 133 C.E., Bar Kokhba (meaning "Son of the Star"), was proclaimed the Messiah and led a revolt spurred on by Rabbi Aqiva, a leading religious authority of the day. Roman forces responded with force, undertook sweeping reprisals, and outlawed Jewish religious observances. The most dramatic and widespread messianic initiative occurred in the seventeenth century. Sabbetai Tzevi (1626–1676), a young kabbalist from Smyrna in Turkey, declared himself messiah at age 22. Driven out by enraged rabbis, he traveled to Salonika, Constantinople, Palestine, and Cairo before returning to Jerusalem with fanfare until he was expelled. Nathan of Gaza (1643–1680), then 20 years old, acted the part of Elijah, the prophet whom tradition expected to be the forerunner of the Messiah. Sabbetai Tzevi returned to Smyrna in triumph in

1

1. *King David enthroned while he plays his favorite instrument, the zither. David is the one who with the greatest force and splendor, personified the royalty of Jewish tradition. Here we see him in a stained glass window by Marc Chagall, in the Cathedral in Metz, France.*

1665. From there his movement spread through Europe. In 1666, under threat of torture and death by the Sultan in Adrianople, he converted to Islam. Those followers who did not abandon his cause sought to make sense of his apostasy by invoking a theory of "sacred sin," going so far as to suggest that the Torah would be brought to its messianic fulfillment only through actions that might appear immoral on their outward surface but, because of their inner meaning and intention, actually accomplished redemption.

In the last decades of the twentieth century, many of the followers of the Hasidic Rabbi M. M. Schneersohn, known as the Lubavitcher *Rebbe*, thought that he might be the messianic redeemer. He sought to renew religious fervor and observance by encouraging them to teach and practice in the public realm in order to persuade less observant Jews to return to religion. His family migrated from Eastern Europe to New York City where he died on June 12, 1994, at age 92. At that time there was expectation that he might lead the chosen people back to the Holy Land. Among some followers there is still high hope that he might somehow return from the grave to do so.

2. The drawing by A. Baldanzi, depicts that which is the symbol of the Sho'ah, a concentration camp for Jews in Nazi Germany during World War II.
3. A religious school in Jerusalem frequented by Hasidim, followers of Schneersohn, whose portrait is seen hanging on the wall.

MYSTICISMS: MERKABAH, KABBALAH, HASIDISM

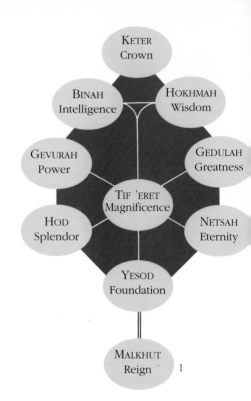

1. Diagram of God's ten divine emanations (sephirot) with their most common attributes. These aspects or qualities or "regions" in which divinity is extended, build the essence of God, and for some, the instruments with which God governs the world.
2. A Yemenite necklace is designed to hold an amulet. These items were often deemed to react through contact with the individual, and transmitted a type of positive emanation. At times they contained formulas of a religious nature that could be recited or represented. The amulet is assumed to be endowed with special powers against evil. Although intended as a protective object, it is often worn solely for decorative reasons. Jewish mysticism has used amulets, often tying them to sacred writings, yet has always warned against the infatuation of using them as a means of easy access to the divine.

MERKABAH. Alongside law and observance, Judaism includes vibrant mystical experiences. Merkabah mysticism is based on extraordinary visions. During the mystical journey, the visionary visits *hekhalot*, seven palaces or halls where heavenly beings dwell, and then contemplates the very throne and chariot of God. There the mystical voyager encounters Metatron, an angel with human characteristics, identified as the Biblical personality Enoch. All those in the family line that descends from Adam to Noah die except for Enoch, whom "God takes" (Genesis 5:18–24) and, according to tradition, raises to the rank of an angel. Metatron-Enoch becomes a focus of mystical and apocalyptic literature. Most *hekhalot* texts date from the third to the sixth centuries C.E., although aspects of Merkabah mysticism date back to the second century B.C.E.

KABBALAH, meaning "tradition" is a different form of Jewish mysticism. The word refers to a special mystical tradition hidden from public teaching. Kabbalists held that God is boundless (*Ein-soph*). However, in the course of creation, a "breaking of the vessels" (*shevirat ha-kelim*) containing the prime matters of darkness and light (evil and good) occurred, and there was a withdrawal or contraction (*tsimtsum*) of God into himself. Kabbalah aims to overcome fundamental divisions and restore—at every level of the heart, soul, and world—the unity that existed among all realities in the beginning. The idea is expressed with great power by Abraham ben Samuel Abulafia (1240–1291), a Sefardim Kabbalist who sought union with God, and by Moses of León (1250–1305), who composed the *Sefer ha-Zohar* (the Book of Splendor), the best known book of the Kabbala. It encourages an allegorical reading of the Bible, discovering the mystical meaning of names and letters. This goal of healing rifts and restoring oneness is called *tikkun* and it is in accord with two other aims of Kabbalah: *kavvanah* (contemplation through meditation); and *devekut* (clinging to God in a mystical union with the divine). Each of these ends serves as a means to the other two. Isaac Luria

(1534–1572) and his disciple Hayim Vitale organized Kabbalistic ideas into an elaborate system.

Kabbalah attunes itself to the mystical dimensions of grammar, numbers, names, tones, and other corresponding realities found in revelatory writings. Letters of the alphabet reveal commandments and the name of God in the written form and also reveal God to the Parasidics (people in a state of mystic delight) on a level of mystic experience. *Hekhalot* literature and the *Sefer Yetsirah* ("Book of Creation" composed around the third or fourth century) provided Kabbalists a basic worldview: ten *sephirot* (corresponding, some say, to the ten commandments, among other realities) make up the universe. Each sphere contains its own modes of being. Taken together, the *sephirot* contain all imaginable forms of existence in this universe. The *sephirot* (and the realities in them) are connect to one another via 22 paths (corresponding to the 22 letters of the Jewish alphabet). Just as letters and numbers can be combined and recombined to refer to one and all kinds of

realities, so also can the mystic enter the transformative power of numbers, letters, names, and signs to contact realities they signify. By uncovering the mystery of the Scriptural text, the Kabbalist unveils the divine light hidden in the words and letters. Recombinations of visible letters correspond to inner changes that enlighten the mystic's entire being in ecstasy. In this way, humans become microcosms reproducing within themselves the macrocosm of the larger world. Humans can become one with all things, including the divine being. Some Kabbalists speculate there are several spiritual universes that sustain one another: 1) *atsilut* (Emanation) made up of ten *sefirot* which, in sum, compose the mythical man Adam Kadmon; 2) *beriyah* (Creation), with the seven mystical palaces (*hekhalot*) and the merkabah; 3). *yetsirah* (Formation) where all the hosts of angels reside; and 4) *asiyah* (Making) which is the perfect, normally invisible, model of the visible world seen by humans. The last years of the twentieth century are witnessing a revitalization of interest in Kabbalah and enthusiasm for mystical experiences predicated on Kabbalistic learning and practice.

HASIDISM. In eighteenth century Poland, Israel ben Eliezer (born around 1700), more commonly entitled Baal Shem Tov or simply Besht, launched a vital religious movement called Hasidism (from the word *hasid*, meaning "pious one"). When rabbinic leaders of Judaism in eastern Europe, such as Elijah of Vilna, condemned Hasidism for not stressing Talmud and

asceticism, Hasidim set up their own synagogues. They ignored the established rabbis and turned to *zaddikim* ("the righteous ones") as their leaders. *Zaddikim* descend from their ecstasies for the benefit of their communities. Using extraordinary powers acquired in their heavenly ascents, they work wonders on behalf of others. Hasidism has spread throughout the Jewish world and is present as a notable influence in Europe, North America, and Israel. Hasidism stresses that God is everywhere and it centers spiritual life over the joy that comes from union with God (*devequt*). Ascent of the soul into God's divine light (*aliyat ha-neshamah*) can occur in the most ordinary activities, even when eating or sleeping. Though Hasidim performs dramatic songs and dances, they hold that directing one's mind toward union with God transforms all physical actions into worship.

3. An imaginary representation of the seven palaces through which, according to the Merkabah mysticism, one has to pass to reach the throne of God.
4. A Hasidic family dressed in holiday clothing, standing in front of the Wailing Wall in Jerusalem.

THE SPECTRUM OF OBSERVANCE

Jewish practices vary by region, family, and the branch of Judaism to which one belongs. Customs cover all aspects of life, from tearing blades of grass and tossing them over one's shoulder at the end of a visit to the cemetery, to covering mirrors or not wearing leather shoes during the seven-day (*shiva*) period of mourning after death. Custom governs greetings, clothing, and prayer. As noted, prescribed behavior is heightened at Sabbath and Holy Days.

Kashrut is a special area of food observances, instructing Jews to avoid restricted foods and to prepare and serve allowable foods properly. The Bible links dietary laws to holiness: "You shall be holy people to me; therefore you shall not eat any meat that is torn by beasts in the field." The Talmud details the complexities of *kashrut* in a special tractate called *Chullin*. Regulations govern ritual slaughter (*shechitah*), examination of the animal and internal organs (*bedikah*), and preparation of the meat (*kashering*). Generally speaking, Orthodox and Conservative Jews today observe standards of *kashrut*. Reform Judaism leaves matters to individual judgement.

The eighteenth century saw change in the relationship between Jews and non-Jews. The 1789 Declaration of the Rights of Man by the French Revolution was symptomatic of the change for it declared all human beings equal before the law, including Jews. Notwithstanding setbacks and anti-Semitism, Jews increasingly faced decisions about how they wanted to relate their social and religious life to that of non-Jews.

As early as 1843 in Frankfurt, Germany, and in the 1870s in America, Reform Judaism introduced new views of worship, observance, and texts. Reform Judaism emphasizes the unity of religion and ethics, dedicating itself to establish peace, eradicate poverty, and achieve social justice. The teachings of

1. A painting representing a eulogy given before the burial of a body in the Jewish cemetery in Prague at the end of the 18th century. The participants are members of the Confraternity of Death, an important association within the populous Jewish community of Prague who assisted in the correct administration of the rites for the dead and dying.

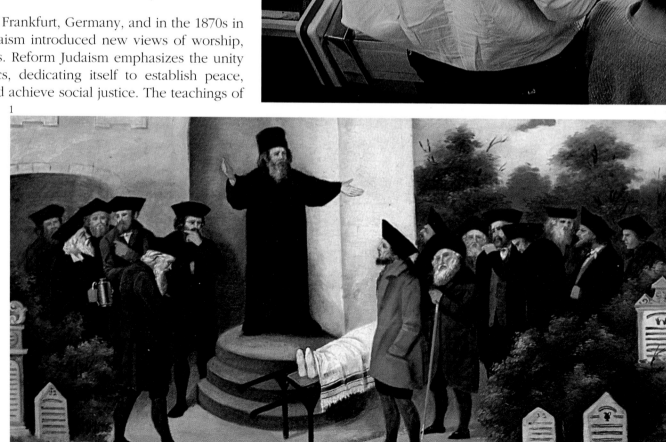

the Torah should remain the source of Reform Jewish life but—and here was the important innovation that opened to change—they should be adapted to the needs of each age

(other works and traditions of interpretation, such as the Talmud, should be diminished in status). Some Reform Jews today believe that their heritage should not be lived in overtly religious practices. Rather, Judaism should be reworked so that the spirit of those historical religious practices yields ethical principles, psychological truths, political commitments, and wisdom, all of which would have universal standing and transform civil society into a just, peaceful, and healthy world that sustains the wellbeing of the common good.

Conservative Judaism was founded by leaders like Sabato Morais and Solomon Schechter, both of the Jewish Theological Seminary in New York (opened in 1886), to conserve traditions set aside by Reform initiatives. In 1918 Mordecai Kaplan established a synagogue in New York as a center for Reconstructionism, a movement that stems from Conservative impulses and yet includes more liberal, naturalistic and anthropocentric philosophies of religion.

Those who observe tradition discuss what accommodations, if any, should be made to modernity in regard to forms of education, engagement with the state, family organization, and even personal hygiene and dress codes. Orthodoxy, associated with the 1896 founding of the Isaac Elchanan Yeshiva (now Yeshiva University), is a numerically strong branch of modern Judaism, although it took shape later than the Reform, Reconstruction, or Conservative branches. Modern Orthodox embrace any cultural benefit that is not expressly forbidden by God's revealed teaching. Other Orthodox reject such accommodation. In turn, others reject Orthodoxy, saying that it is undemocratic and anti-intellectual, unwilling to work with science and history. Still, the distinctive religious life of Judaism is not being irreversibly eroded by modern society. On the contrary, many Jews (and some gentiles) whose families were unacquainted with strict observance rediscover observant Jewish religious life, for example, when they move from their secular homes to attend secular colleges and encounter lively traditional practices through the Hillel house on their college campus. There is lively ferment at every level of Jewish culture today, a search for the meaning of Torah. Notwithstanding differences, all branches of Judaism embrace plural forms of response to God's revelation and election. On the one hand, they cling to the Covenant made with Moses on Mount Sinai by keeping the Torah and, on the other hand, they hold fast to the messianic promises granted to King David on Mount Zion. Keeping Torah and living in hope of promised salvation, Jews know they collaborate with God in redeeming the world.

2. A self-service restaurant for kosher food in a district of Jerusalem. The word kosher means suitable or fit and indicates food that has been prepared in a ritually fit manner according to Jewish tradition. These types of restaurants can be found throughout the world and display the word kosher both inside and out, as we can see here.
3. A street in the ghetto in Toledo, Spain, where men of letters and culture were influential, during the reign of Islam and during the reign of the Catholic Kings, with whom the Jews eventually were in conflict and by whom the Jews were eventually banned during the 15th century.

THE *SHEMA*: A PRAYER FOR ALL TIME

Hear, O Israel! The Lord is our God, the Lord alone. You shall love the Lord your God with all your heart and with all your soul and with all your might. Take to heart these instructions with which I charge you this day. Impress them upon your children. Recite them when you stay at home and when you are away, when you lie down and when you get up. Bind them as a sign on your hand and let them serve as a symbol on your forehead; inscribe them on the doorposts of your house and on your gates.

(Deuteronomy 6: 4-9)

If, then, you obey the commandments that I enjoin upon you this day, loving the Lord your God and serving Him with all your heart and soul, I will grant the rain for your land in season, the early rain and the late. You shall gather in your new grain and wine and oil.

Therefore impress these My words upon your very heart: bind them as a sign on your hand and let them serve as a symbol on your forehead, and teach them to your children reciting them when you stay at home and when you are away, when you lie down and when you get up.

(Deuteronomy 11: 13-14, 18-19)

The Lord said to Moses as follows: Speak to the Israelite people and instruct them to make for themselves fringes on the corners of their garments throughout the ages; let them attach a cord of blue to the fringe at each corner.

Thus you shall be reminded to observe all My commandments and to be holy to your God. I the Lord am your God, who brought you out of the land of Egypt to be your God: I, the Lord your God.

(Numbers 15: 37-38, 40-41)

Here are selections from the *Shema*, an ancient prayer of special power and prominence in Jewish life. The *Shema* is composed of three Biblical passages (Deuteronomy 6: 4-9; 11: 13-21; Numbers 15: 37-41). Jewish men are required to recite the *Shema* twice each day, morning and evening. Individuals recite it before sleeping and on the brink of death. For thousands of years the *Shema* has been the last word on the lips of Jewish martyrs, who followed the example set by Rabbi Akiva, martyred in the second century. A ruling in that same century obliged Jewish parents to teach the *Shema* to their children as soon as they began to say their first words.

1. *A family joined together in Seattle, on the West coast of the United States, to celebrate Pesach or Passover. The dinner, Seder, follows specific rules in remembrance of the pact the Jews made the night before leaving Egypt where they had lived as slaves under the Pharaoh. It was the eve of the exodus to the Promised Land.*

2. 3. *Columns, capitals, and arches in the historic synagogue in Toledo, Spain, act as the backdrop for the present-day Stieblach Synagogue in Jerusalem where several faithful are already praying while others enter.*

1

GLOSSARY

words in CAPITALS *are cross references*

Aggadah   The non-legal aspects of Judaism that include theology, ethics, stories, and parables.

Anti-Semitism   Prejudice and hostility against Jewish people and Judaism.

Ark   In this book, the term refers to the cabinet where the TORAH scrolls are kept in the synagogue. It is the most sacred place in the synagogue. The term applies also to the ARK OF THE COVENANT and to the ark in which Noah, his family, and the ancestors of all living beings took refuge during the universal flood.

Ark of the Covenant   The chest which was built by the ancient Jews to hold the tablets of the COVENANT.

Ashkenazi   A Jew whose family originated in Central or Eastern Europe. Named after Ashkenaz (Genesis 10:3).

Circumcision   This ritual, first practiced by Abraham as part of the COVENANTAL relationship between the Jewish people and God, removes the foreskin of the penis.

Conservative Judaism   Modern movement that holds that changes in traditional Jewish life are acceptable and inevitable in modern times, but that the history and traditions of Judaism remain very important. Conservative Jews try to conserve as much tradition as possible, but believe that changes may be made to ensure the vitality of Judaism for all people.

Covenant   Agreement or treaty between two parties; the promise between God and the Jewish people on which the Jewish people base their religion.

Diaspora   Refers to the fact that Jewish people live all over the world, in separate communities apart from each other, instead of all together in one place as in ancient times.

Halakhah   All of the Jewish Law, in the broad sense of religious norms, observances, and communal practice, from Scripture to recent rulings by rabbis. Halakhah is rooted in God's revealed will.

Hasidism   Movement of piety founded by wandering popular preachers, especially Israel ben Eliezer Baal Shem Tov, in the late eighteenth century in Eastern Europe. It emphasizes that one should find joy and union with God in everyday life. A spiritual leader called a *zaddik* usually leads the Hasidic.community.

Hellenistic   Term describing the culture and ideas found in the Roman Empire between Alexander the Great (fourth century B.C.E.) and emperor Constantine (fourth century C.E.). During this time, the Greek-influenced culture of the Romans mixed with the culture of the conquered people of the area, resulting in a new culture that was a blending of many types of ideas, religions, and art.

Kashrut   Rules concerning which foods may or may not be eaten, and how they should be prepared.

Lubavitcher   Also known as Habad, it is a branch of mystical HASIDISM that is based in Brooklyn, NY, though originally from Belarus via Latvia and Poland. The Lubavitchers preserve traditional piety and hold that divinity is present throughout the universe. They integrate modern techniques into the bounds of Jewish Law, under the direction of the rebbe.

Midrash   Rabbinical writings that are interpretations of the Bible. They help people to understand the stories, prophecies, and other parts of the Bible. Midrash can also mean the particular way the rabbis study the Bible in order to correctly interpret it.

Minhag   Customs of the Jewish community. These can be as important as the HALAKHAH, and sometimes can even be preferred over it.

Minyan   The group of at least ten men that is required to form a community for worship in a synagogue.

Mishnah   The oral Law as written down by the rabbis. It includes rules for worship and everyday life and it is divided into six parts. It was first written down and organized at the beginning of the third century C.E.

Mitzvot   Commandments, duties, responsibilities, or good deeds that Jews must fulfill after they have undergone their *bar mitzvah* ceremony.

Mysticism   Special and extraordinary religious experiences which are by definition difficult to describe because they are nothing like the everyday experiences most people have. Mystics often receive knowledge that people cannot receive in normal study or experience.

Observance   Following the Law, obeying the will of God by participating in a ceremony or ritual, or fulfilling the obligations of Judaism in other ways.

Orthodox Judaism   Modern movement that was founded as a reaction to the REFORM JUDAISM. Orthodox Jews believe that Jews must follow the Law completely, and believe that the TORAH and Law are God-given.

Passover (Pesach)   On this feast, the Jewish people remember their liberation from captivity in Egypt by celebrating with a *Seder*, a ritual dinner.

Pentateuch   The first five books of the Hebrew Bible: Genesis, Exodus, Leviticus, Deuteronomy, and Numbers. The Pentateuch as we know it was composed after the destruction of the Temple in 586 B.C.E. It begins with God's creation of the world and traces the history of His holy people Israel up until the COVENANT God established with them through Moses on Mount Sinai.

Rabbi   An ordained teacher, he is the spiritual leader of his community, and studies and interprets the TORAH.

Reconstructionism   Modern movement founded by Mordecai Kaplan that understands Judaism as a religious civilization changing and evolving through history, but always remaining committed to the continuation of the Jewish people and values.

Reform Judaism   Modern movement, grown out of the European Enlightenment, that tries to adjust Judaism to the present world. Reform Jews focus more on the moral and ethical aspects of Judaism, and less on the observance of all the rules of the HALAKHAH.

R'osh ha-Shanah   The Jewish New Year. It occurs in September because the Jewish religious calendar is different from the calendar used in the secular world.

Sefardim   A Jew whose family originated in Portugal or Spain (called Sefarad as mentioned in Obadiah 1:20).

Shiva   The customary seven-day mourning period after a death. During this time, the bereaved stay home to receive visitors.

Talmud   Means "learning." Talmud is a compilation of commentaries on the MISHNAH. It is an authoritative source of Jewish tradition, and deals with both HALAKHAH and AGGADAH.

Torah   Refers to both the Hebrew Bible (especially the first five books), and all the teaching that comprises the Jewish tradition as well as methods of inquiry about them. Since the teaching and interpretation that make up part of the Torah are always being added to, the Torah is not just the story of what happened to a group of people thousands of years ago. The Torah remains revelatory to new generations of Jews through time.

Yom Kippur   The Day of Atonement. On this day, Jewish people ask God's forgiveness for whatever wrongs they have done during year.

Zionism   Movement dedicated to the creation of a homeland for the Jewish people. Throughout their life in the DIASPORA, Jewish people hoped and prayed for a return to the land of Israel. In the late nineteenth century, Theodor Herzl began the modern Zionist Movement in order to promote the political establishment of an independent Jewish nation.

BIBLIOGRAPHY

BLOCH, ABRAHAM P. *The Biblical and Historical Background of Jewish Customs and Ceremonies.* KTAV Publishing House, New York, 1980.

CHOURAQUI, ANDRÉ. *Il pensiero ebraico* ("Jewish Thought"). Queriniana, Brescia,1989.

ELIADE, MIRCEA, ed. *Ebraismo* ("Judaism"), vol. 6 from the *Enciclopedia delle Religioni* ("Encyclopedia of Religions"). Jaca Book, Milan (in preparation).

FACKENHEIM, EMIL L. *To Mend the World: Foundations of Post-Holocaust Jewish Thought,* 1st Midland ed. Indiana University Press, Bloomington, 1994.

FOHRER, GEORG. *Storia della religione israelitica* ("Story of the Israelite Religion"). Paideia, Brescia, 1985.

GLAZER, NATHAN. *American Judaism,* rev. 2nd ed. University of Chicago Press, Chicago, 1989.

IDEL, MOSHE. *L'esperienza mistica in Abraham Abulafia* ("The Mystic Experience in Abraham Abulafia"). Jaca Book, Milan, 1992.

___. *Hasidism: Between Ecstasy and Magic.* State University of New York Press, Albany, 1995.

___. *Cabbalà. Nuove prospettive* ("Kabbalà. New Perpectives"). La Giuntina, Florence, 1996.

KUGEL, JAMES. *On Being a Jew: What Does It Mean to Be a Jew? A Conversation About Judaism and Its Practice in Today's World.* Harper San Francisco, San Francisco, 1990.

LEVENSON, JON D. *Sinai and Zion: An Entry Into the Jewish Bible.* Winston Press, New York, 1985.

LIEBERMAN, SAUL. *Studies in Jewish Myth and Jewish Mysticism.* State University of New York Press, Albany, 1993.

NEUSNER, JACOB. *Il Giudaismo nei primi secoli dei Cristianesimo* ("Judaism in the First Centuries of Christianity"). Morcelliana, Brescia, 1989.

___. *The Mishnah: Introduction and Reader.* Trinity Press, Philadelphia, 1992.

RUDAVSKY, D. *Modern Jewish Religious Movements: A History of Emancipation and Adjustment,* 3rd ed. Behrman, New York, 1979.

SCHOLEM, GERSHOM G. *Le origini della Kabbala* ("The Origins of the Kabbalah").Edizioni Dehoniane, Bologna, 1990.

SELTZER, ROBERT M. *Judaism: A People and Its History.* Macmillan, New York, 1989.

SOLOVEITCHIK, HAYM. *Rupture and Reconstruction: The Transformation of Contemporary Orthodoxy.* Rabbinical College of America, Yeshiva University,1994, pp. 64-130.

TRUTWIN, WERNER. *Il mondo delle religioni: Ebraismo, Cristianesimo, Islamismo, Induismo, Buddhismo* ("The World of Religions: Judaism, Christianity, Islam, Hinduism, Buddhism"). Jaca Book, Milan, 1998.

WOLFSON, ELLIOT R.. *Through a Speculum That Shines: Vision and Imagination in Medieval Jewish Mysticism.* Princeton University Press, Princeton, 1994.

INDEX